The Joy of Piano Entertainment

Compiled and arranged by Denes Agay.

Yorktown Music Press

Exclusive distributors:
Hal Leonard
7777 West Bluemound Road, Milwaukee, WI 53213
Email: info@halleonard.com

Hal Leonard Europe Limited
42 Wigmore Street Marylebone, London, WIU 2 RY
Email: info@halleonardeurope.com

Hal Leonard Australia Pty. Ltd.
4 Lentara Court Cheltenham, Victoria, 9132 Australia
Email: info@halleonard.com.au

Printed in the EU.

Sleepers Awake

Theme from *Cantata No. 40*

Johann Sebastian Bach

Baroque Fanfare

Jean Joseph Mouret

Moderato con moto

Jesu, Joy Of Man's Desiring

Johann Sebastian Bach

Andantino

Theme from Piano Concerto
K. 467

Wolfgang Amadeus Mozart

Themes from "Rustic Wedding" Symphony

1. In the Garden

Karl Goldmark

2. Bridal Song

Intermezzo

Romance
from the opera *The Pearl Fishers*

Georges Bizet

España

Lively waltz

Emil Waldteufel

I Love You

EDVARD GRIEG

Serenata
Rimpianto

Enrico Toselli

Hungarian March

from *The Damnation of Faust**

Hector Berlioz

Moderately; with vigor

*Traditional melody, known as "Rakoczy March", named after a 17th century Hungarian revolutionary leader.

D.C. al Fine

Echoes of Vienna

"Tales from the Vienna Woods"- Johann Strauss

"My Life Is Love and Pleasure"- Joseph Strauss

"Radetzky March"- Johann Strauss, Sr.

Allegretto

Nola

Felix Arndt

Chiapanecas

(Hand Clapping Song)

Mexican Folk Dance

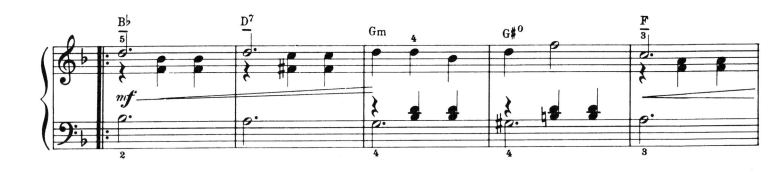

Hava Nagila

Bright tempo (Hora)

Israeli Folk Dance

Caprice No. 24

Niccolo Paganini

Joplin Gems

Themes from *The Entertainer, Solace, Original Rags*

Scott Joplin

Very slow "Solace" (A Mexican Serenade)

Lively "Original Rags"

Polka Italiana
"Oh, Marie"-"Funiculi, Funicula"

Arranged by
Gerald Martin
Very lively

E. di Capua
L. Denza

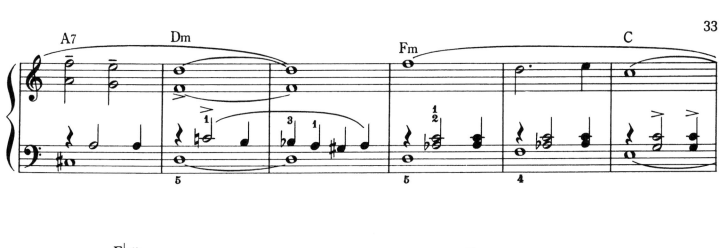

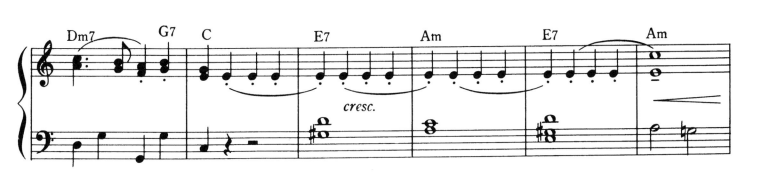

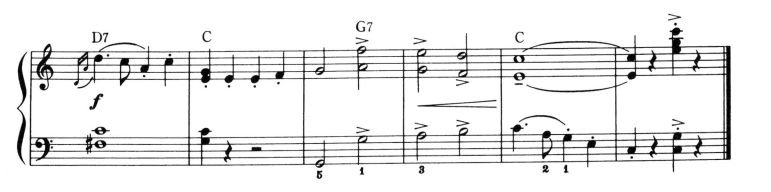

March of the Toys

from *Babes in Toyland*

Victor Herbert

Little Rhapsody on Gypsy Tunes

Moderato; freely

Gerald Martin

"The Sleeping Beauty" Waltz

Lively waltz tempo

Peter I. Tchaikovsky

*Lower octaves are optional

Music Box Rag

Denes Agay

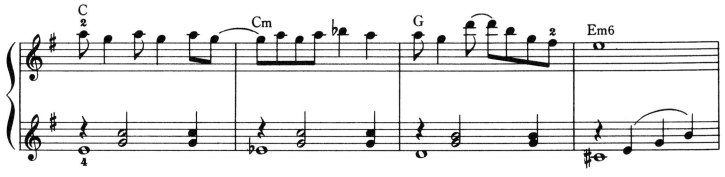

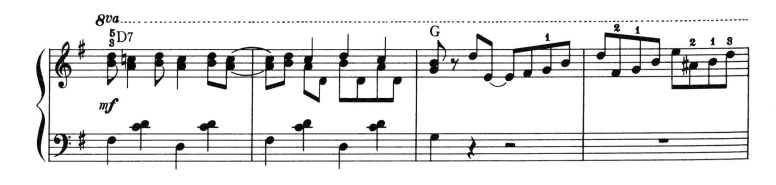

The Marionette's Funeral March

Charles Gounod

Jazzy Little Brown Jug

Gerald Martin

Clair de Lune

Slowly, with expression

Claude Debussy

Romance

ANTON RUBINSTEIN

The Washington Post

John Philip Sousa

Lively march tempo

Slavonic Dance No. 10

Anton Dvorak

Freely moving

Farandole
(from L'Arlesienne Suite No. 2)

Georges Bizet

Tarantella Napoletana

Italian Folk Dance

The Memory Waltz
(Danube Waves)

JAN IVANOVICI

Strolling At Loch Lomond

Leisurely, with a solid beat

Gerald Martin

The Boll Weevil Boogie

Folk Tune

Chicken Reel

Traditional Fiddle Tune

Alabama Hoe Down

R. J. HAMILTON

Hesitation Waltz
from the ballet *The Red Poppy*

Reinhold Glière

Slow waltz tempo

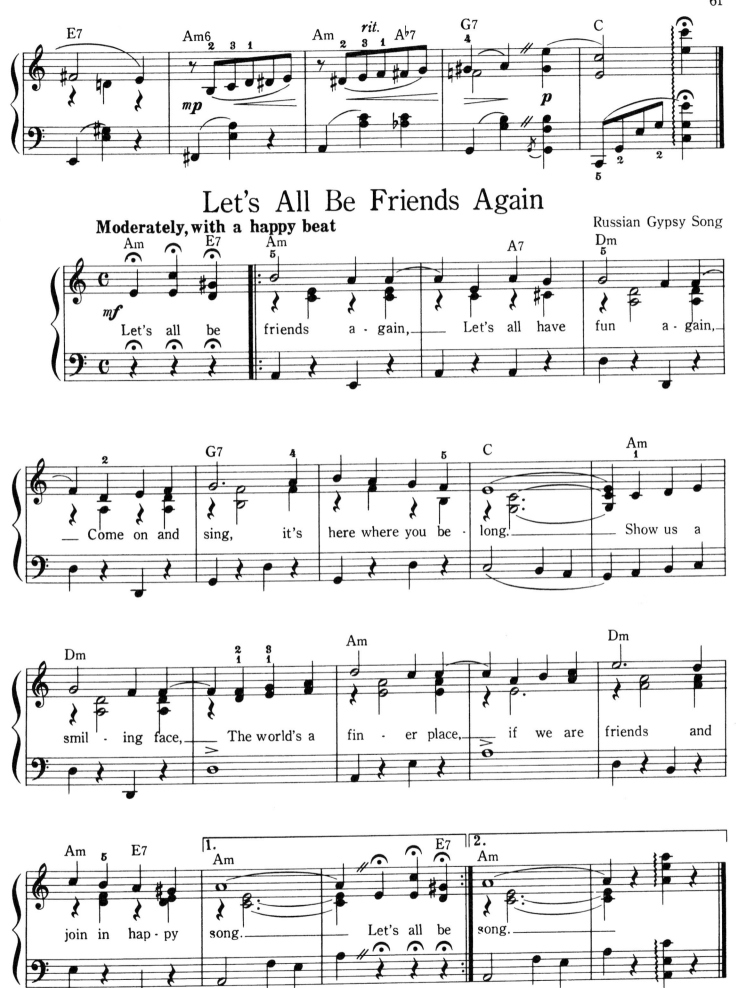

Let's All Be Friends Again

Moderately, with a happy beat

Russian Gypsy Song

Let's all be friends a - gain,___ Let's all have fun a - gain,

___ Come on and sing, it's here where you be - long.___ Show us a

smil - ing face,___ The world's a fin - er place,___ if we are friends and

join in hap - py song.___ Let's all be song.

I Am The Very Model

from *The Pirates of Penzance*

William S. Gilbert

Arthur Sullivan

A Wand'ring Minstrel

from *The Mikado*

William S. Gilbert

Arthur Sullivan

I Have a Song

from *The Yeomen of the Guard*

William S. Gilbert

Arthur Sullivan

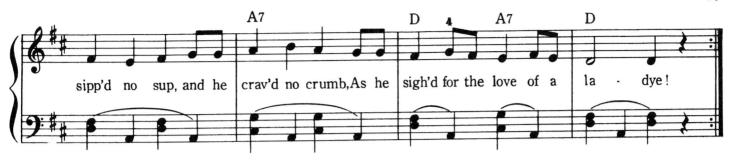

sipp'd no sup, and he crav'd no crumb, As he sigh'd for the love of a la - dye!

Lovely Evening

(Round)

Moderately slow

Traditional

Oh, how love - ly is the eve - ning is the

eve - ning, When the bells are sweet - ly ring - ing, sweet - ly

ring - ing Ding, dong, ding, dong, ding, dong!

Morning Has Broken

Gaelic Melody

2. Sweet the rain's new fall
   Sunlit from heaven,
   Like the first dew fall
   On the first grass.
   Praise for the sweetness
   Of the wet garden,
   Sprung in completeness
   Where his feet pass.

3. Mine is the sunlight,
   Mine is the morning,
   Born of the one light
   Eden saw play.
   Praise with elation,
   Praise every morning,
   God's recreation
   Of the new day!

Amazing Grace

Folk Hymn

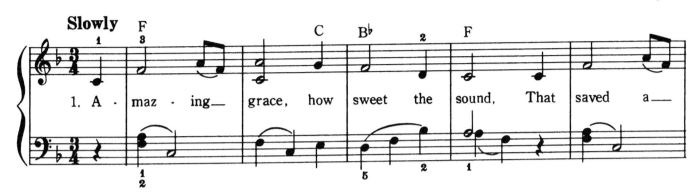

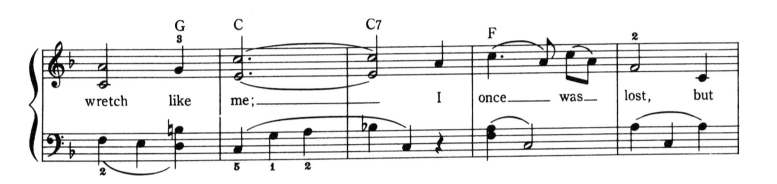

2. 'Twas grace that taught my heart to fear,
   And grace my fears relieved;
   How precious did that grace appear
   The hour I first believed.

3. Thro' many dangers toils and snares,
   I have already come;
   'Tis grace that bro't me safe thus far,
   And grace will lead me home.

4. How sweet the name of Jesus sounds
   In a believer's ear;
   It sooths his sorrows, heals his wounds,
   And drives away his fear.

5. Must Jesus bear the cross alone
   And all the world go free?
   No, there's a cross for ev'ry one
   And there's a cross for me.

The Big Rock Candy Mountain

Folk Song

Bill Groggin's Goat

Moderately

Traditional

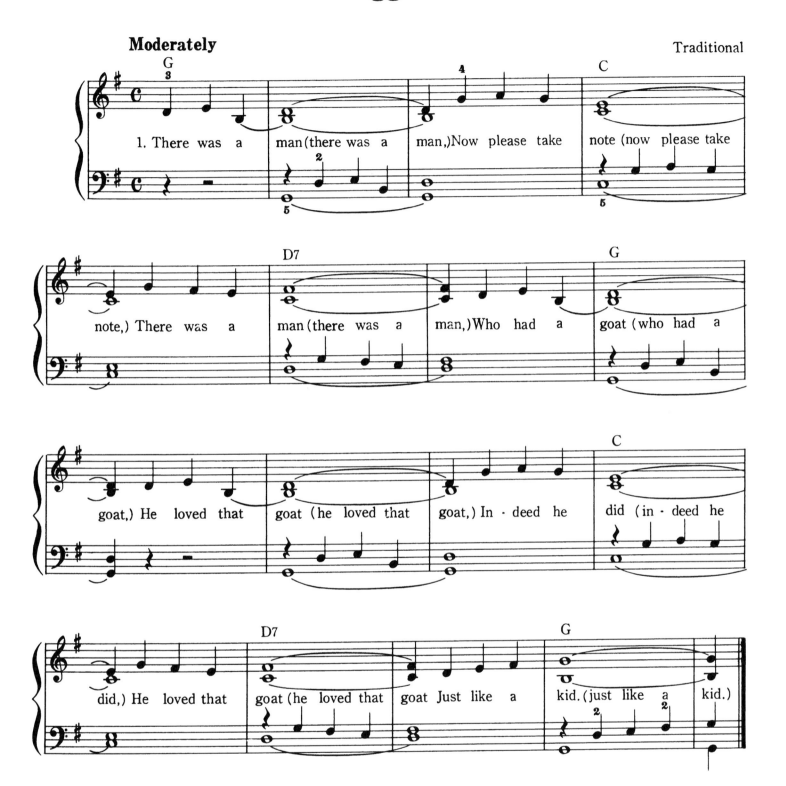

2. One day the goat
   Felt frisk and fine,
   Ate three red shirts
   Right off the line.
   The man he grabbed
   Him by the back,
   And tied him to
   A railroad track.

3. Now when that train
   Hove into sight,
   That goat grew pale,
   And green with fright.
   He heaved a sigh,
   As if in pain,
   Coughed up the shirts,
   And flagged the train.

Auprès de Ma Blonde

FRENCH FOLK SONG
arr. by Denes Agay

Comfortable, lilting tempo

Vive L'Amour

Traditional

Lively

Let ev - 'ry good fel - low now join in a song, Vi - ve la com - pa -

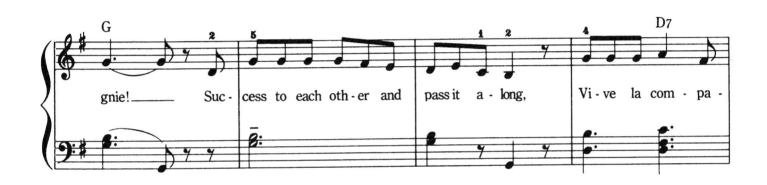

gnie! _____ Suc - cess to each oth - er and pass it a - long, Vi - ve la com - pa -

gnie! _____ Vi - ve la, vi - ve la, vi - ve l'a - mour, Vi - ve la, vi - ve la,

vi - ve l'a - mour, Vi - ve l'a - mour, Vi - ve l'a - mour, Vi - ve la com - pa - gnie!

This Old Man

Play Tune

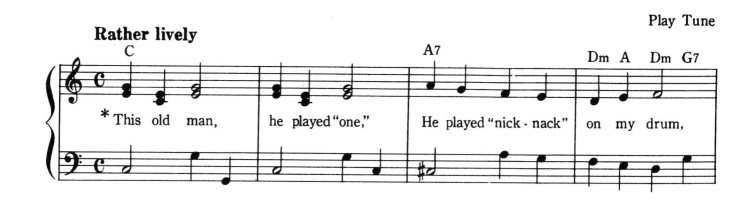

Make up your own rhymes for the successive numbers, "two" to "ten."

Tell Me Why

Traditional Song

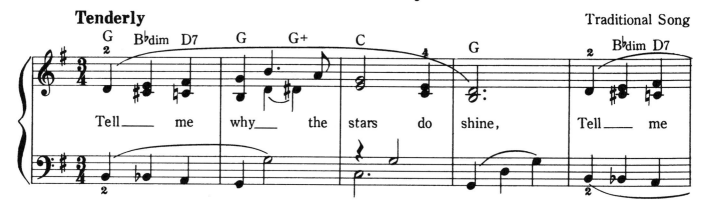

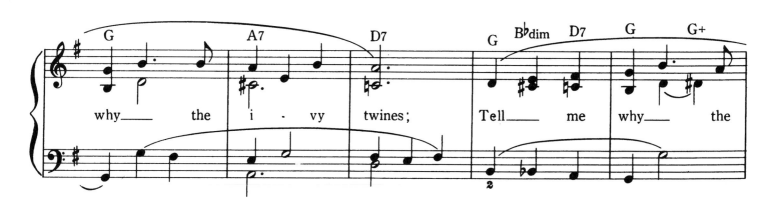

skies are blue, And I will tell you why I love you.

Michael Finnigan

Play Tune

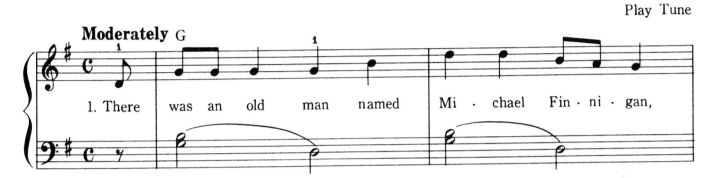

1. There was an old man named Mi - chael Fin - ni - gan,

He grew whisk - ers on his chin - i - gin, The wind came up and

blew them in a - g'in, Poor old Mi - chael Fin - ni - gan, be - gin a - g'in.

2. There was an old man named Michael Finnigan
   He got drunk through drinking ginnigan,
   That's how he wasted all his tinnigin,
   Poor old Michael Finnigan, begin ag'in.

3. There was an old man named Michael Finnigan
   He grew fat and then grew thin ag'in,
   Then he died and had to begin ag'in,
   Poor old Michael, please don't begin ag'in.

Sweet Betsy From Pike

Moderately bright

Folk Song

Did you ev-er hear tell of sweet Bet-sy from Pike, Who cross'd the wide

prai - ries with her lov - er Ike? With two yoke of ox - en, A

big yal - ler dog, A tall Shang - hai roost - er, And one spot - ted

hog. Hoo - dle dang, fol - de - dye - do, hoodle dang, fol - de - day.

Swiss Hiking Song

Traditional Swiss Tune

Come and take a walk with me, Hol - di - ri - dee - a, hol - di - ri - a,

Come and sing a song with me, Hol - di - ri - dee - a, hol - dee - a.

High and low we'll go, Hol - di - ri - dee - a, hol - di - ri - a,

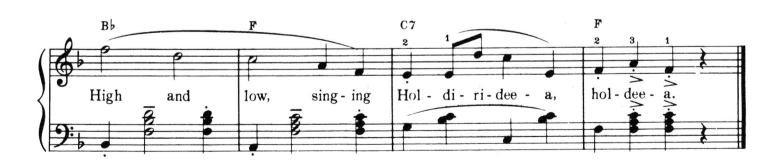

High and low, sing - ing Hol - di - ri - dee - a, hol - dee - a.

The Animal Fair

Rise And Shine

Play Tune
(Based on a Spiritual)

1. Rise ___ and shine ___ and give God the glo-ry, glo-ry,
Rise ___ and shine ___ and give God the glo-ry, glo-ry,
Rise and shine and give God the glo-ry, glo-ry, Chil-dren
of the Lord. Lord.

2. God said to Noah, there will be floody, floody (twice)
Get your children out of the muddy, muddy,
Children of the Lord.

3. Noah, he built him, he built him an arky, arky, (twice)
Made it out of hickory barky, barky,
Children of the Lord.

4. It rained and rained for fo-orty days-y, days-y, (twice)
Drove those couns'lors nearly crazy, crazy,
Children of the Lord.

5. The sun came out and dried up the landy, landy (twice)
Everyone felt fine and dandy, dandy,
Children of the Lord.

He's Got The Whole World In His Hands

2. He's got the wind and the rain in His hands,
   He's got the wind and the rain in His hands,
   He's got the wind and the rain in His hands,
   He's got the whole world in His hands.

3. He's got the tiny little baby in His hands,
   He's got the tiny little baby in His hands,
   He's got the tiny little baby in His hands,
   He's got the whole world in His hands.

4. He's got you and me in His hands,
   He's got you and me in His hands,
   He's got you and me in His hands,
   He's got the whole world in His hands.

When The Saints Come Marchin' In

Traditional

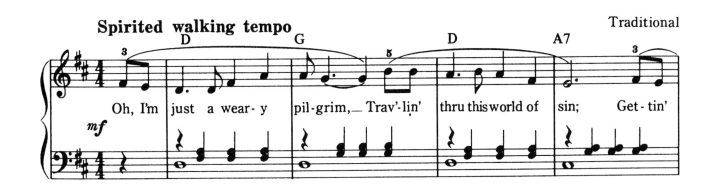

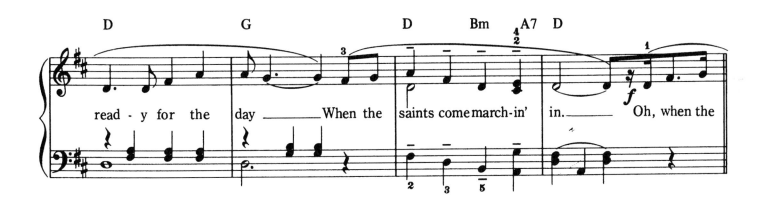

Sweetly Sings The Donkey
(Round)

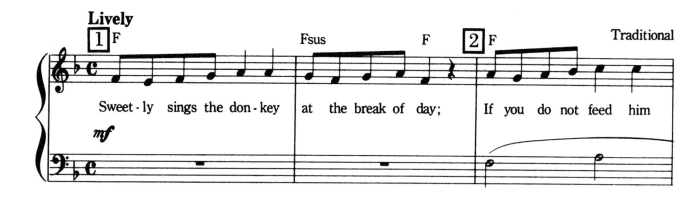

Sweet-ly sings the don-key at the break of day; If you do not feed him

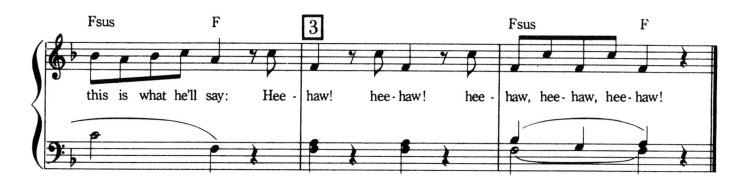

this is what he'll say: Hee-haw! hee-haw! hee-haw, hee-haw, hee-haw!

Row, Row, Row Your Boat
(Round)

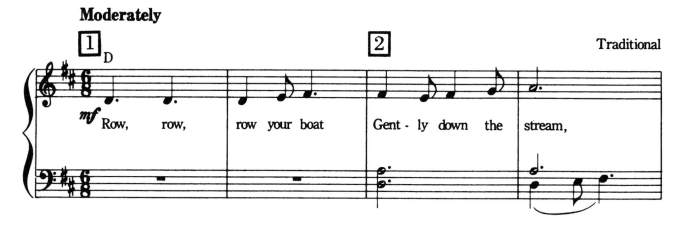

Row, row, row your boat Gent-ly down the stream,

Mer-ri-ly, mer-ri-ly, mer-ri-ly, mer-ri-ly, Life is but a dream.